Working Big

Working Big

A Teachers' Guide to Environmental Sculpture

John Lidstone/Clarence Bunch

VNR VAN NOSTRAND REINHOLD COMPANY
New York Cincinnati Toronto London Melbourne

Van Nostrand Reinhold Company Regional Offices:
New York Cincinnati Chicago Millbrae Dallas
Van Nostrand Reinhold Company International Offices:
London Toronto Melbourne

Designed by the authors
Photographs by the authors unless otherwise credited

Published by Van Nostrand Reinhold Company
A Division of Litton Educational Publishing, Inc.
450 West 33rd Street, New York, N.Y. 10001

16 15 14 13 12 11 10 9 8 7 6 5 4 3 2 1

Library of Congress Cataloging in Publication Data

Lidstone, John.
  Working big.

  Bibliography: p.
  SUMMARY: Discusses the child's natural inclination
to "work big" and suggests large-scale art activities
including some in the new air art.
  1. Art—study and teaching (Secondary)—United
States. 2. Air Art. [1. Air art. 2. Art—Technique]
I. Bunch, Clarence, joint author. II. Title.
N363.L5   707'.12'73   74-15716
ISBN 0-442-24795-8

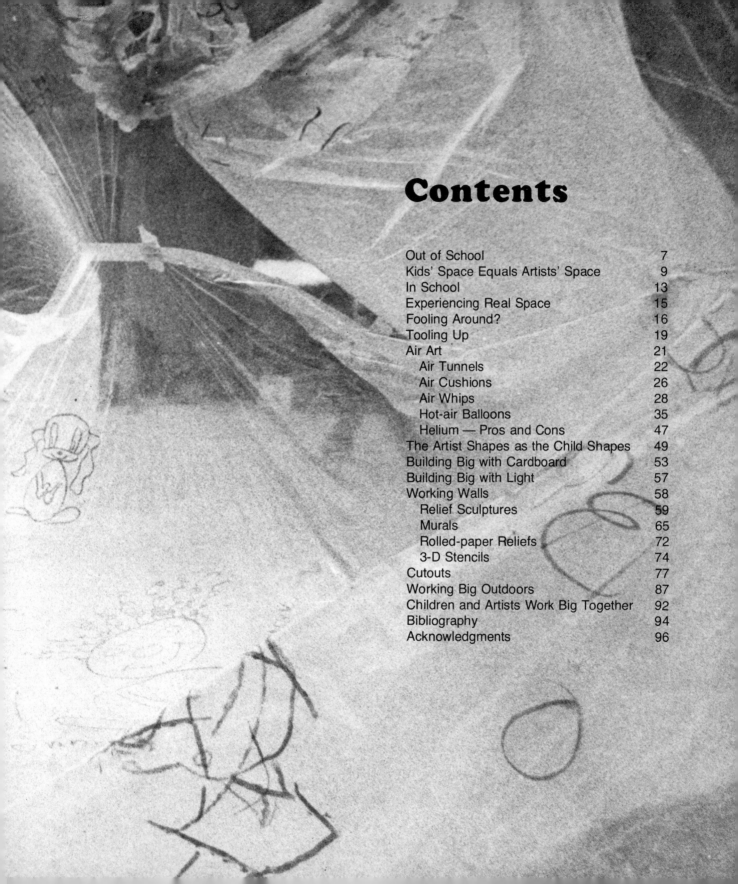

Contents

Out of School

The child explores his physical world with complete abandon. On his own, when the barriers are down and nothing stands between him and his curiosity, he experiences his environment with an enthusiasm that adults have long forgotten. Whether he is in the country or in the inner city, he savors the electric sensuality and excitement of each day. He seems to have limitless resources for seeking out enjoyment and satisfaction.

His explorations of natural space are expansive and wide-ranging. He never walks when he can run; he makes a game out of getting from one place to the next — every errand has its delightful detours; he crouches with bent-kneed curiosity to study the industry of an ant; he cranes back to speculate on the shapes of clouds; he flattens his face against the window of the subway car to get as close as possible to the tunnel streaking by. With an exuberant leap to touch a low-hanging branch or a kick at a can, he celebrates his physical well-being as he senses his place in the world around him. Only the artist and the child can claim such a rich and easy empathy with life.

Robert Smithson, *Broken Circle/Spiral Hill,* 1971–72. Earth in water. Diameter: 140 feet.

Kids' Space Equals Artists' Space

When nature itself provides the medium, children are eager and intuitive artists. They need no one to tell them that the moist grittiness of sand is just right for sculpturing or that damp snow can be squeezed into the most satisfactory shapes. A pile of paving blocks immediately triggers construction ideas; discarded tires, an event. Bicycling freely back and forth across the concrete surface of a schoolyard, children consciously create superdesigns with wet wheels; complicated systems of canals and dams reveal their attempts to trap the tide; even a lawn mower is pressed into service to create artistic swaths en route to completing its job. There is such an easy expansiveness to children's artistic use of space outdoors that the fact that some have trouble filling a 9-inch-by-12-inch sheet of manila paper in the classroom seems incongruous. Their enthusiasm for working big outdoors and their facility with whatever materials are at hand point out yet another example of how children on their own delight in ordering space in ways not dissimilar to those favored by many contemporary artists.

Robert Smithson, *Amarillo Ramp,* 1973. Red sandstone and shale with veins of white caliche. Length: 396 feet; diameter: 150 feet (top), 150–160 feet (base); width: 10 feet (top), 10–30 feet (base); elevation: up to 12 feet, depending on the level of the lake.

The creative abilities and enthusiasms of the child are never more fully satisfied than when he is working with natural or found materials in an unstructured situation. When there are no space limitations; when techniques do not impose restrictions; when the child, through his own exploration of the forces and materials involved, decides on his own way of working; when total physical preoccupation is possible, the child is revealed as a consummate artist in his own right. Observing youngsters work in this way leads to the inevitable conclusion that for children art is play and play is art.

When the child grasps the creative possibilities of a material or a process, he is predisposed toward it in the same way that he is excited by the prospect of playing in the sand or in the snow. This excitement soon diminishes if restrictions are imposed or if tasks are assigned that bewilder him or are incompatible with his own ideas. Conversely, excitement is maintained when media and techniques match the child's capabilities and he can work freely to establish his own goals. In other words, the more art in the classroom is like play, the more effective it is likely to be.

When children initiate their own activities, they are more often than not group-oriented and eventlike. Play is inevitably more important than product, and creativity is centered as much in what to do as in how to do it. Children's play with blocks, for example, illustrates this, and similar behavior can be observed in much older children when they manipulate more sophisticated modules of one kind or another.

Large-scale activities in school tend to involve groups and to be event-centered, and therefore they are more playlike and real than traditional classroom activities. Teachers are continually confronted by children in the art room who don't know what to do or can't think of an idea. Yet these same children function effectively as creative individuals in a natural play group. This fact in itself suggests that *working big* is well worth trying as a classroom strategy.

David Ligare, *Sand Drawing #2,* 1971. Pencil. 11 inches by 9 inches. (Collection of Gordon Crispo)

In School

The child is as eager to explore the world of art as he is to explore the real world outside the classroom. He is as enthusiastic about participating in art activities as he is about the rough-and-tumble of after-school play. In fact, in his initial school years art activities are play to him, and art materials are as exciting as anything he encounters out of school.

However, sustaining this high level of natural involvement in art becomes more and more difficult as each school year gives way to the next. As they grow older, children inevitably become dissatisfied with their attempts to portray reality on paper. Art materials that were once exciting become old hat, and exploration begins to lose its point. Even with the best teaching, cognition imperceptibly takes precedence over feeling and intuition; intellectual examination, over physical experience; and the art room becomes just another academic classroom.

Working Big offers two solutions to this dilemma. The first is to introduce the teacher to ways in which he or she can involve students in activities on a large enough scale to make art a reality rather than a desktop exercise. The second is to suggest means, quite removed from the process/product orientation of the everyday art program, by which students can intensify their awareness of the real physical world from which, after all, the elements of art are derived.

Experiencing Real Space

No matter what area of art an artist is involved in, he is confronted with the problem of space. A painter is concerned with spatial relations on a two-dimensional surface; an architect deals with functional aspects of space; a sculptor must be aware of the space surrounding his piece as well as its internal spatial qualities.

To enjoy art or to participate effectively in an art activity, we must not only have a sense of aesthetic space but also be excited by the artist's or our own handling of space.

The child's artistic interpretation of space is a developmental phenomenon. At first, he is not concerned about the relationship in space of the objects he draws — he creates freely and with gusto. Later, he desperately wants to make such relationships "real," but, because he cannot understand or cope with the conventions of portraying three-dimensional reality on a two-dimensional surface, he is frustrated, fails, gives up, and in most cases never draws with joy and conviction again.

The limitations of the conventional art room, once students leave the lower grades, make it one of the least effective places to learn about space and classroom activities the least productive approach to help-ing students understand what space is all about. Undoubtedly, there is much to be said for varying classroom routine with work outside its formal constrictions, and for the teacher or the youngsters creating situations in which they can become involved in real-space experiences. In fact, many of the art experiences we hope children will enjoy as adults, such as architecture, happenings or events, and sculpture, rely on a heightened awareness of real space if the participant is to fully appreciate them.

One way to make the break — to have classroom activity become more like out-of-school activity, more like life itself, and so more effective — is to *work big*. This is not to suggest that we turn our backs on such undeniably valuable approaches to art as drawing, painting, and design but that we do not hesitate to work with big or real materials or to become involved in physically big activities when it seems that they will best fire students' imaginations and provide the most fruitful learning situations. No desk-top approach will engender the excitement about space or yield more personalized knowledge about it as an art element than building a cardboard maze, for example, and exploring its restricting length, or discovering the spatial euphoria of a plastic bubble you have helped construct yourself.

Fooling Around?

Traditionally, art is object-oriented. The artist creates *things* — paintings, pots, sculpture, films — that are meant to have lasting significance. Even though art education focuses attention on the *process* rather than on the *product,* classroom art, like most art in general, is concerned primarily with the skills, techniques, and imagination used in the production of art objects and secondly with the appreciation of those art objects singled out as particularly praiseworthy.

Many contemporary artists and art educators who oppose this view of art are now reexamining this static position. The critic Willoughby Sharp, in a recent article in *Studio International,* maintained: "Art's enemy is the object. Reality is events, not objects. Static structures are anachronisms. They are irrelevant to today's cultural and technological situation. . . . Reality is energy, not things. Object art is over".

While we as teachers may not want to adopt such an advanced position as Sharp's or may not be prepared to abandon our reliance on the role of process/product as the principal determinant of creative development, we might well take note of the importance of *objectless* activities in an age in which it is difficult to define in absolute terms what constitutes an "art object" or, in fact, what "art" itself is. Many of us profess to appreciate a work of art because we judge that it conforms to the conventional art-appreciation standards. We are baffled, however, as soon as we are confronted

with a situation that purports to be art but gives out none of the traditional signals, or a situation in which we must physically participate in the creation, in effect, of our own art, objectless or otherwise.

We are similarly baffled, once we leave behind the reassuring guideposts of traditional art, as to what is a meaningful art activity and what is not. The youngsters pictured here are reacting to prepared spatial situations; they look suspiciously as if they are merely fooling around if we compare their behavior to that of others of the same age engaged in, say, a painting lesson. But even a traditional art object like a painting does not begin on the canvas. It is not created in a vacuum but rather evolves out of feelings and experiences. The children we see here are involved in physical activity calculated to span the gap between imagination and reality.

So much art from the upper grades is hackneyed and repetitious that we sometimes wonder whether we have missed a step along the way. Piaget's observations indicate that memory in children is very closely tied to physical action. It is likely that a child's reactions to enclosure and freedom as he romps through a controlled environment fix in his memory concepts of space that he could not arrive at within the limitations of the classroom or through the traditional art activities carried on within it. Body-spatial experiencing may result in a greater understanding of two-dimensional, pictorial space when at a later time the child is desperately endeavoring to depict the real world in his drawings and paintings. In the light of these considerations we should not dismiss the fact that "fooling around" can have immediate aesthetic value.

Tooling Up

Large-scale projects are so eye-catching and dramatic that it is understandable to assume that they are achieved with unusual and hard-to-get materials. The truth is that working big basically involves little more than traditional classroom supplies and equipment plus large-scale industrial castoffs such as cardboard boxes, long cardboard tubes, lengths of discarded plastic, packing materials, and packaging supplies.

In fact, good-quality trash is the very best resource for working on a large scale, and children, being natural scavengers, are the world's best collectors. Some very worthwhile projects require nothing more than just such found materials — for example, a giant-sized sculpture built from old automobile tires — while more complex undertakings might demand rolls of polyethylene or a handsaw. Elementary-school classes, obviously, will not require the more sophisticated equipment and supplies that would be appropriate to a high-school program.

Here are some items other than throw-aways and some sources of supply that are commonly used by teachers to "work big."

Polyethylene, clear, 100-feet-by-14-feet rolls, .004 MIL (for tunnels)	Ain Plastics Inc. 65 4th Avenue New York, N.Y. 10003
Polyethylene, clear, 100-feet-by-20-feet rolls, .010 MIL (for air cushions)	Ain Plastics Inc.
Polyethylene sleeving, extruded, clear, .0015 to .0019 MIL (buy by the pound)	available at commercial plastic-bag manufacturers or Colonial Transparent Products Co. 870 South Oyster Bay Road Hicksville, N.Y. 11801
Vinyl-coated nylon fabrics (for large air cushions)	Smith-Dixie Industrial Fabrics North Side Drive Box 1203 Statesville, N.C. 28677
Valves for small inflatables	Roberts Valves Halkey-Roberts Corp. Spring Valley Ave. Paramus, N.J. 07652 (write for catalog)
Plastic adhesive tape (Monsanto), 100 feet by 2 inches	Local hardware stores or Monsanto Co. Kenilworth, N.J. 07033
Blowers (for air whips)	Electric Trading Co. 313 Canal St. New York, N.Y. 10013 (blowers may be rented from commercial fan companies)
Weather balloons	Edmund Scientific Co. 623 Edscop Building Barrington, N.J. 08007
Helium, small containers (12.1-liter aerosol cans)	Edmund Scientific Co.
Helium (larger containers)	Toy Balloon Corporation 204 E. 38th St. New York, N.Y. 10016
Austrian Tissue (all colors), 29 inches by 20 inches	Austen Display Inc. 133 W. 19th St. New York, N.Y. 10011
Tissue-paper glue	R. J. Sisk Co. New London, Conn.
Styrofoam sheets	CCM Arts and Crafts Inc. 9520 Baltimore Ave. College Park, Md. 20740
Corrugated cardboard, single- and double-faced, 50-foot rolls	Local paper dealers or Bernhardt Zinn Paper Co. Inc. 30 Great Jones St. New York, N.Y. 10012
Cardboard sheets, all sizes, 2-ply to 6-ply	same
Cardboard boxes, all sizes	same or as found materials
Dressmakers' buckram, white, 4 inches wide	Regent Fabrics 122 E. 59th St. New York, N.Y. 10022
Honeycomb boards (70 inches by 40 inches) Homosote panels (8 feet by 4 feet) Sterno stoves and fuel Lengths of stovepipe Hammers Handsaws Pliers Nails Sandpaper Paint	Local hardware stores
Skilsaw model no. 487, two-speed, ¼-inch jigsaw type (with large-toothed blade)	Local hardware stores or Skil Corporation 5033 Elston Ave. Chicago, Ill. 60630
Masking tape, 1 inch wide Scotch tape, ¾ inch wide Gun-type stapler Staples Large T-square 42-inch steel ruler Spotlights (with reflectors and clamps) Elmer's Glue	Local art-supply dealer

Air Art

"Air is of all classical elements the one that is the least explored by artists (yet it) offers more new possibilities than the other elements" (Otto Piene, *More Sky* [Cambridge: M.I.T. Press, 1973], p. 2). Air is such a commonplace part of life that we are seldom aware of its existence except perhaps to complain that it is dirty and to contemplate ways to clean it up. We have taken the air for granted in the past, and even today give little or no thought to it in terms of art. We have thought of sculpture for a long time as surrounded by air, by space, and interacting with it, but until very recently we have stopped short of acknowledging the fact that air itself can be an integral part of sculpture.

Air art is brand-new — new not only technologically but as an attitude that symbolizes a new movement. To borrow Otto Piene's words, it moves away from "the art world" toward a "world of art." Most air art is transient: a delicate smoke sculpture, subject to the whims of wind and weather, is experienced only once. Even a more permanent air structure like a balloon is usually seen only for a short period, then deflated, packed up, and stored away for a future event. In a way it resembles its contemporary counterpart, the electronic image, which is screened, then stored to await future viewing. In contrast to statuary and painting, air art is not the stuff that museums are made of; it is more at home as sky art, environmental art, atmospheric art; it gives us the same momentary pleasure as a sunset or a cloud. Air art, too, is often the product of many minds and hands and is associated with participation and activity, so it is at the same time people art, social art, public art.

Balloons, air whips, air tunnels, air cushions, air ribbons, kites, bubbles, wind sculptures, flags, banners, skywriting, and smoke sculptures are forms of air art; some are new, some traditional. All are current forms of artistic expression, but as yet they play little or no role in the classroom, although each has much to offer in terms of the creative development of children. The fact is that air forms have been neglected in the curriculum, not so much because they are difficult to plan and execute, for, in fact, they pose few problems for the teacher, but because they do not easily fit the traditional static, permanent, object-oriented concept of an art activity.

There must be a constant interchange between art itself and school art if art education is to be vital and alive and if education as a whole is to fit the child for the age in which he lives. Working with air-art materials and forms not only opens up new avenues of expression to the child but helps us as teachers to understand the elements of such contemporary art forms as the event, conceptual art, objectless art, and transient art, which are foreign to many art rooms and which appear almost as antiart to the uninitiated. Once the child and teacher become involved in the excitement and exhilaration of space play or in the construction and contemplation of an undeniably beautiful piece of air sculpture, however, there is a good possibility that we will become more relaxed in our attitude toward what art is and less apprehensive about an art activity that swings outside the accepted norm based on traditional values.

Otto Piene, *A Field of Hot-air Sculptures Over Fire in the Snow,* 1969. Thirty differently shaped transparent polyethylene balloons, controlled by strings and raised repeatedly by heated air emitted from the nozzles of ten propane-gas tanks spaced around the field. Diameter: 3–30 feet; length: 10–100 feet. Illumination: two 20-kilowatt arc lights.

Air Tunnels

An air tunnel is sculpture. An air tunnel is environment. An air tunnel is experience. Because of these ambiguities, an air tunnel can be a rich art resource for the teacher.

From the outside, an air tunnel, with the sun glinting off its glistening contours and the surroundings mirrored in its rounded surfaces, is an impressive and compelling sculptural form. Inside it is a magical world, always refreshingly clean and more than often cool; what is outside, even in the meanest neighborhood, is experienced as pleasantly distorted color shapes so that reality seems a million miles away. This magical feeling of unreality is heightened by the fact that exterior sounds are muffled and that light is softer, milky, diffuse, different from what we ordinarily experience.

Looking out, the child is only vaguely conscious of people. Are they real? Can they see him? Many children believe that, once in the tunnel, they are invisible and behave accordingly. "It's like floating on air," one child says. "It's like being inside a snake," exclaims another. Such reactions are unique and true.

A tunnel provides a different architectural experience from what we are used to. There are no right angles; a tunnel may be so long and the light so diminished that we do not see its end. The walls give when touched; up close they are transparent; step back and they appear translucent and insubstantial — yet at the same time the inside experience causes us to feel as if we were cloistered and in complete privacy.

Because the space within the tunnel is so equivocal and so dramatically different from what he normally experiences, the child reacts to it and copes with it in an inventive, exuberant, physical way. He uses the space as an art element with which to express himself.

Although large and seemingly complex, air tunnels require only easy-to-obtain materials and are surprisingly simple to construct. With a standard 100-foot-by-14-foot roll of .004-MIL-thick polyethylene, 2-inch clear, adhesive plastic tape, and an ordinary window fan, preferably 22 inches by 22 inches or larger, you can construct a tunnel that will be 5 to 6 feet high when fully inflated.

To make an air tunnel of this type:

Unroll the plastic on a level surface. It is packaged so the two outside edges are next to each other. Tape these two edges together to form a tube, tape one end closed, and tape the open end to the outside frame of the fan, pleating it to get the best closure. Turn on the fan and let it inflate the tube to its maximum fullness.

Cut a vertical slit in the wall of the tunnel approximately 3 feet from the fan; it should be just long enough from top to bottom to serve as the entrance and exit. Smooth on a 6-inch length of tape crosswise at the bottom of the slit and another at the top to keep the wall of the tunnel from splitting. If a student stands at the entrance to let participants in and out, it is usually unnecessary to construct an air lock. An effective one can be made, however, by taping a broad polyethylene strip 5 to 6 inches longer than the slit just above the slit

inside the tunnel so the air is blowing against it.

Since polyethylene is a fairly tough plastic, an air tunnel can be deflated, rolled up, stored, and used over and over again. Rips or tears can be easily and effectively patched with the same clear adhesive tape that was used to assemble the original structure. A tunnel can be almost fully inflated even if there are extensive holes and tears in its walls, because the rigidity of the structure depends on a steady stream of air passing through it, unlike a balloon, which is filled with static air.

There is no need to be apprehensive about the safety of an air tunnel, because, even if the fan were to fail, enough residual air would remain to support the walls for a considerable time. The polyethylene is no threat either, as it is on the one hand too heavy to cling to a child's face like a plastic laundry bag, and on the other hand it is light enough for a youngster to put his finger through it easily.

Tunnels can be moved around to form shapes that differ radically from a basic, straight-line design. Tunnels can also be joined to form mazelike configurations or extremely large sculptural forms such as the eight-story inflated tower shown here, which was built by students at New York City's Collegiate School.

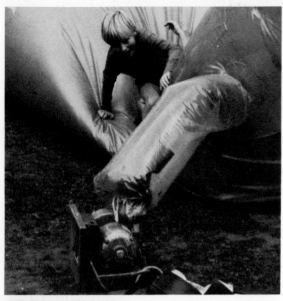

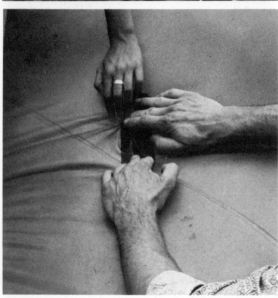

Air Cushions

Art is, as life is, basically concerned with the physical world. All the arts are involved with physical sensation. The more we are alive to sensation, the more art means to us. Having children simply make art objects or learn about the work of other artists is not to give them a complete art education. We must alert them to the physical world of which art is a part and out of which man-made art emerges. So far we have concentrated most of our teaching energies into involving the child in such physical areas of art as color and two-dimensional space. We have done little to awaken him to the experience of real space. We have directed our attentions toward involving him in art process and art appreciation without at the same time creating situations in which he could experience spatial sensation and realize his own body as an instrument of creative expression.

Air cushions allow us to work toward both of these ends by providing a physical environment with which the child can realize his own physicality and experience himself as a dimension of the real-space environment.

An air cushion is constructed in the same manner as a tunnel except that any openings that might allow air to escape must be sealed up carefully. The poly-ethylene employed must be a much heavier gauge (at least .010 MIL) to stand up to the physical demands of children climbing and bouncing on the exterior.

Air Whips

Most air-sculpture projects involve the child not only in making an art object but in the physical activity connected with it. An air whip combines making and doing into a simultaneous experience.

An air whip is a form of kinetic sculpture that is most intriguing to students, and its construction is quite within their capabilities. It is exciting because of its unpredictable, erratic, darting movements, which, although harmless, are quick and snappy enough to enliven its surroundings. Children react to an air whip with the same frenetic delight that they exhibit when dodging the stream from a garden spray or playing crack-the-whip.

The excitement generated by an air whip is heightened by the fact that the air rushing through its plastic tube creates loud, cracking, popping sounds. Because the sound, regardless of the intricacies of its rhythm, is generated by brisk movement of the sculpture itself, there is a perfect orchestration of sound and movement, which is largely responsible for the effectiveness of an air whip as kinetic expression.

Flashing in the sun or scintillating at night in the glare of floodlights, air whips, particularly if there are more than one and if they are quite long (they can run as much as 100 feet), can be fantastically beautiful.

To make an air whip:

1. Slip one end of the sleeve over the exhaust vent of the blower. The other end is left open for the air to escape. The escaping air causes the whip to whip about in the sky.

2. Fasten the sleeve to the blower with 2-inch tape (Monsanto Plastic Tape was used here) so the seal is both airtight and strong enough to prevent it from pulling free when the blower is turned on and the sleeve begins to whip around.

Air whips are the simplest possible air structures to make; all you need are a blower, extruded plastic sleeving, and adhesive plastic tape. The more powerful the blower, the better. An ordinary fan won't work, because the air doesn't move fast enough or with enough force. An ideal blower for air whips is one with a small, lipped opening so plastic sleeving can be attached with ease. The most workable plastic is .002-MIL-thick polyethylene, since it is not too heavy or too light; use a sleeve form that has been extruded so it has no seams.

3. There is no way to predetermine the most effective length, since it depends upon the force of the pump, so it is best to work with a generous amount of sleeve, cutting it back (perhaps more than once) until you are satisfied. If the sleeve is cut too short, the full potential of the whip will not be realized.

4. The same plastic tape used to fasten the sleeve to the blower can be used to repair any rips that occur during use. Sleeves can be used over and over again and are best stored each rolled into a tight package.

1

2

3

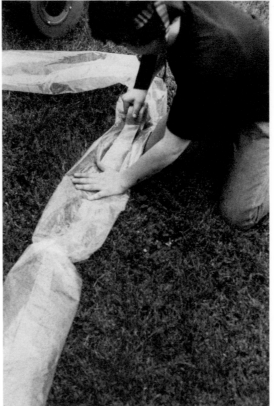

4

If the length of the sleeve matches the power of the blower, the whip fully extends itself and can be manipulated with ease. The air tends to escape through the sleeve in puffs, creating a marked rhythmic pattern.

Squeezing or patting the sleeve changes the rhythm and adds to the variety of movements and sounds made by the whip. Even quite young students quickly become adept at manipulating air whips and are fascinated by the endless variety of sounds and configurations created. Dramatic results can be obtained by using more than one whip at a time; whips of different lengths will create different patterns, sounds, and speeds. Colored smoke, confetti, or other lightweight elements can be introduced into the fan so they pour out at the top of the sleeve to add spectacular dimensions to an already exciting activity.

Hot-air Balloons

Although a balloon was reputed to have been flown by the Greeks in 500 B.C. the first true hot-air balloon was not launched until 1783. Designed and built by two French paper manufacturers, Jacques Étienne and Joseph Montgolfier, it measured 33 feet in diameter. Filled with hot air from a straw-and-wood fire, it rose to a height of 1,500 feet.

In 1972, the first World Hot-air Balloon Championship was held in Albuquerque, New Mexico, with close to one hundred balloons from seventeen countries competing. Although featuring the latest in propane burners and envelopes made from high-tenacity nylon, all the balloons at Albuquerque bore a marked resemblance to the original Montgolfier balloon that predated them by almost two hundred years. This similarity exists because the basic design of these balloons is determined by the buoyant nature of hot air.

Now, as then, the envelope of the balloon is made up of a number of gores or divisions, which, when stitched together, form the characteristic pear-shaped air chamber we associate with hot-air balloons. The tissue-paper balloons shown here and on the next few pages owe their lifting power to hot air and are made up, as are today's sport balloons, of gores, so they are, in fact, true hot-air balloons.

1 2

3 4

To make a tissue-paper hot-air balloon:

1. Make a template to serve as the pattern for the gores by taping together single sheets of newspaper to the desired size.

2. Fold the newspaper in half lengthwise. Tape or pin it against a wall with the open side down. Pin the ends of a piece of string at the upper corners of the newspaper. Allow the string to find its own curve (no deeper than the paper will allow) by gravity.

3. Adjust the string so that on the left-hand side it leaves a stem approximately 3 inches long by 2 inches wide, which will become the top of the balloon. On the right-hand side leave a much wider stem, approximately 6 inches long by 4 inches wide. (When the paper is unfolded, the stems, of course, will be twice as wide.) As a rule of thumb, the stem at the bottom of the gore should be twice the length and twice the width of the stem at the top. A larger balloon will have larger gores and longer and wider stems, but the ratio between them should remain the same.

4. Once the string is adjusted, trace its path with a black Magic Marker.

5. Take the paper down from the wall without unfolding it and cut along the drawn line.

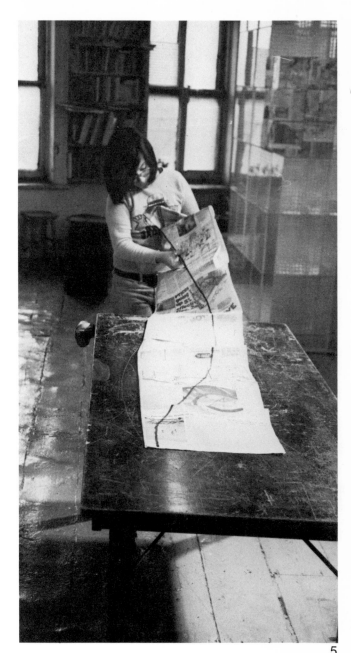

5

6 7

8 9

6, 7, 8. Tissue-paper sheets usually do not come in large enough sizes to make a gore. You will probably have to glue several sheets end to end to make a panel large enough for your purposes. This can be done in much the same way as the newspaper sheets were joined together, except that glue is used instead of tape. A good solution can be made by mixing equal parts of Elmer's Glue and water. Even better is Sisk Tissue Collage Glue, which is especially prepared for tissue paper.

By arranging the sheets of tissue paper in a certain order, a color pattern can be worked out to enhance the appearance of the balloon. For example, if the second sheet in each panel is yellow, the balloon will have a yellow stripe running around it when all the gores are glued in place.

9. As each tissue-paper panel is completed, it should be stored so it will not be crushed. A simple way is to pin (not tape) the panels to a bulletin board or wall. If such a surface is not available, the panels can be folded loosely and piled on top of one another. Notice how narrow bands of colored tissue have been glued across some panels in the photograph above. When the balloon is complete, these will form stripes that will encircle the inflated balloon in the same way that larger panels form larger stripes.

10

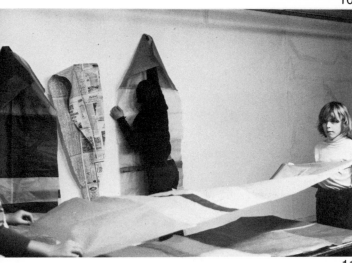

11

10, 11. When the tissue-paper panels are complete, they are stacked flat one on top of another. It is difficult to make a successful balloon with less than six gores. Naturally, the more gores you have, the larger the circumference will be. Here eight gores are used, which is probably the most effective number for a school balloon.

12. When all the panels are stacked and the edges matched one with another, they should be stapled at several points along the edges to keep the tissue paper from shifting.

12

13 14

16. Using fairly large scissors, cut out the gores. Make sure to cut through all eight layers of tissue paper.

14. Now you are ready to glue. Glue the first gore to the second with either of the glues mentioned in step 6. (No matter how many students are involved, they should work on only one side of the balloon at a time.) You will need to work quickly, so it is best to have one student brush on the glue while another presses the sheets together carefully to avoid wrinkles.

18. Then move to the other side of the balloon and glue the second gore to the third. Alternate back and forth until all the gores are glued together except the edge of the first and the opposite edge of the last. Bring the unglued edge of the first gore past all the other gores to meet the unglued edge of the last. At the same time, fold the other gores back on themselves to allow the edges of the first and last gores to be brought around them to fit flat against each other, enclosing the other gores.

19. Glue the edges of the first and last gores together.

16

13, 14. Center the template on top of the stacked tissue-paper panels. Trace around its edges with the black Magic Marker. (If two students work together, one can hold the template in place while the other traces.)

15. After the tracing is complete, lift the template off but do not throw it away, because it can be used to make other balloons of the same size and shape.

15

17

18 19

20. The "package" thus created has a fish shape, which is the most effective form for a hot-air balloon.

21. When all the gores are glued together, tie the open stem at the top of the balloon with twine. Leave a loop to use for launching.

22. The stem at the bottom must also be left open for hot air to enter and fill the balloon. Some type of durable adhesive tape should be folded over the tissue paper so that the edges of the opening are strengthened and made more rigid. Some balloon makers use a circle of very light wire to stabilize the opening.

20

21 22

23. Each seam must be checked and any gaps closed either by regluing or with tape. Although it is not absolutely necessary, the balloon can be checked further by reversing the motor of a vacuum cleaner and filling it so that any structural defects can be spotted before the balloon is actually flown.

24, 25. Although it is not absolutely necessary, the balloon can be checked further by reversing the motor of a vacuum cleaner and filling it so that any structural defects can be spotted before the balloon is actually flown.

23

24 25

To launch the balloon:

1. Before the balloon can be flown, it must be filled with hot air. Typical sources of heat are a small fire of twigs and shavings, Sterno, charcoal briquettes, or a propane-gas burner. To ensure that none of the heat is wasted, the bottom stem of the balloon should be slipped over a metal sleeve such as a length of stovepipe (as in the illustration) or a column of tin cans whose tops and bottoms have been removed and which are then taped or soldered end to end.

2. To construct a launching pole (see below), simply fasten an S-shaped hook made from soft wire to the end of a bamboo rod or fishing pole. When you are ready to fly your balloon, insert the hook into the twine loop at the top and hold the balloon upright.

3. Because these hot-air balloons are made of very lightweight tissue, rips and tears are inevitable. They can be easily repaired with Scotch Tape, however, and flown again.

1

2

3

The balloon shown at bottom, right was built by a group of students in Albuquerque, New Mexico. A circle of wire was used to make the bottom stem rigid. Unlike the other balloons shown, the aperture was held above a column of coffee cans rather than slipped over them. A wood fire produced a steady supply of very hot air, in contrast to the less intense heat supplied to the other balloons, which depended on a small Sterno stove.

Although students become very caught up in the excitement of launching and flying their balloons, once a balloon is in flight, they are invariably struck by its beauty. Soaring gracefully above them with the sunlight illuminating the colors of the tissue, a hot-air balloon is unusually beautiful. It is air sculpture that is eye-catching and exciting. It is kinetic sculpture too, and balloon making and balloon flying are art events in the truest sense.

Helium — Pros and Cons

As soon as we begin to work in air sculpture, the possibility of creating air-filled forms that can float in space becomes intriguing. To make such sculpture, however, either hot air or a gas lighter than air, such as helium, must be employed. Helium is preferable in several respects, as it creates an effective buoyancy, is non-inflammable, and eliminates the need for a heat source.

Every child has delighted in playing with a helium-filled balloon on the end of a string. But we all know that the balloon quickly loses its airborne quality. The helium does not leak through a loosely tied knot; it slowly escapes through the wall of the balloon. This is just one of the many difficulties a teacher will encounter if helium is used to create air sculpture. It is also extremely expensive, and a great deal is required to fill even a rather modest air structure. Moreover, ordinary plastics will not contain helium at all; only Mylar or rubber (both far from cheap) can be depended upon to hold it for any appreciable length of time.

This is not to say that, when funds or materials are available, helium-filled forms cannot be exciting, as the accompanying illustrations show. Worthwhile events, both meaningful and lots of fun, can be centered in activities that require modest amounts of helium. For example, postcards can be attached to balloons of various colors that ask anyone who finds one of the balloons to return it to the school from which it was launched. This is an exciting activity, beautiful to observe, and it can tell children a great deal about air currents and stimulate their curiosity about the geographical relationships of one place to another. A contemporary version of the note in a bottle, which intrigued many of us as youngsters with the phenomenon of water currents, this sort of activity seems to have an ageless fascination.

Helium-filled balloons in a confined space such as an air tunnel can add another dimension to our appreciation of how the artist is able to transform an environment.

Francisco Sobrino, *Structure Permutationelle E. S. 1,* 1970. Stainless steel. 20 inches by 20 inches by 20 inches.

The Artists Shapes as the Child Shapes

Building is a common activity for any child. Building a design, for example, is invariably a more relaxed and natural activity for him than creating a design on paper. When working with real materials that he can move around, the child appears to have little difficulty in summoning up a vision of a self-conceived three-dimensional structure. Once he understands the nature, possibilities, and limitations of whatever he is working with, a youngster tends to proceed with sureness and at a relaxed but fairly rapid rate toward his goal. The more specific the material, the more deliberate he will be in the construction of whatever it is he has in mind.

Even in nonobjective sculpture architectural demands invariably influence construction so that the child plays the weight of one building element against another. To keep his project upright, he achieves a natural order that pulls his overall design together in a way that would never happen on paper, where "balance" is a formality. When the building components are so big that the completed construction is as big or bigger than the child working on it, the need for good architectural design is emphasized, and the child becomes increasingly aware not only of the structural design of his construction but of its aesthetic design as well.

Rigid materials are particularly effective in stimulating the child's imagination in this way: wooden blocks, Erector set parts, balsa wood strips, and cardboard boxes are good examples of materials with high motivational possibilities. These materials impose their own limits, so the child tends to work within uninhibiting constrictions, particularly in regard to balance, which helps to predetermine a happy outcome for his efforts. This is not necessarily true of such materials as clay, which allow the child to work without restrictions but which often disappoint him because they are not physically able to support his creative ideas.

When the child and the sculptor allow themselves to be guided by the nature of the materials they are working with, they come to amazingly similar artistic conclusions. This is particularly true of rigid media, where parallel restrictions shape the expression of both artist and youngster.

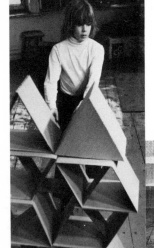

Cardboard boxes immediately suggest to a child all sorts of things he can do with them. He can hide in a box or slide down a hill in it. He can combine boxes to make a fort or a maze. Children will, on their own, find ways to handle even the biggest cardboard boxes. A box large enough to hold a refrigerator or a mattress suggests to a young child a house, a bus, or a boat; an older youngster sees in smaller boxes modules that can become three-dimensional designs. Boxes are play objects, but since children are unconscious artists, their play takes on an aesthetic character, and boxes become an effective sculptural medium.

The ten-year-old shown on these pages first sizes up the possibilities of a pile of cardboard-box shapes left over from a previous project, then combines them in all sorts of ways that are meaningful to him. Finally, he arrives at what he feels is an ultimately satisfying conclusion. As in most play-type activities it is obvious that he is not working from some preconceived notion or extrinsic conception; his ideas grow directly from the material at hand. His inventiveness is tempered by the nature of the forms he works with, but he is not inhibited by them. At every point the challenge of organizing his structure while at the same time making it hang together architecturally makes the ongoing process every bit as exciting as the prospect of accomplishing whatever conceptual goal he may have in mind.

Building Big with Cardboard

Before he begins a new piece, the sculptor must decide what scale will be most effective for his proposed work idea. The same subject matter will have a very different impact on the viewer if it is presented dramatically larger or smaller.

Likewise, scale is important to the success or failure of a classroom project. Unfortunately we are not always as aware of the implications of scale in the classroom as the artist is in his studio. Sometimes large-scale projects are avoided because they take up an inordinate amount of classroom space. More often than not both teachers and students assume that the messiness of a project and the amount of time needed to complete it are in direct relation to its size. Because of this not unreasonable thinking, classroom projects are often small, timid, and ineffectual rather than daring, bold, and satisfying.

In fact, the choice of material, rather than dimension, determines how practical a project is for school. The cardboard boxes we see here are just right for larger than usual classroom sculptural activities. Not only are they a practical solution to a classroom problem, but, because each box is a fair-sized element in itself, even a disorganized pile of boxes will suggest a large-scale solution to an art problem in a way that small-scale materials obviously would never do. Cardboard boxes, particularly if they are discarded, are nothing special to the student. As they are on the borderline of a waste material, the student feels that he can work in a free and easy manner with them. They do not inhibit his expression in the way that a recognized art material might.

As the child's cardboard-box sculpture takes shape, its impressive dimensions give a new context and a fresh value to the material so that he now sees the boxes as a viable medium rather than utilitarian and ordinary.

Creating three-dimensional forms in real space or manipulating real-space elements is quite a different business from creating illusionistic forms on a two-dimensional plane. Building sculpture larger than yourself gives rise to quite different feelings about space than those engendered by work restricted to desk-top dimensions.

Large-scale classroom sculpture immediately suggests a host of problems to the teacher. The sculpture activities with cardboard boxes illustrated here, however, are clean, inexpensive, and easy to organize. Because the boxes can be collapsed, they need only minimal storage space and, of course, can be used over and over again.

Students who have difficulty in comprehending the significance of the three-dimensional modality in traditional activities invariably come to life when confronted by the same problems in a real-space situation. Those who find little satisfaction in small-scale activities are often captivated by the bigger-than-life challenge of activities similar to the ones pictured here.

Working with modules of their own devising, which can be stacked and restacked, ordered and reordered, students can create designs in which the only mistakes are architectural ones. Once the basic unit is established, the students will perceive a certain design logic that not only articulates form but ensures structural vality. When students build quickly without using any other materials besides the cardboard itself, design ideas become design realities in quick order.

Because the elements are so easy to manipulate, students are seldom satisfied with mundane solutions but respond to the challenge of creating exciting forms that require precise positioning of each unit within the whole. As this type of activity is a direct experience, a student who may take three or four periods to produce a two-dimensional design on paper will, especially working with a partner, often create several very creditable cardboard sculptures within a single period.

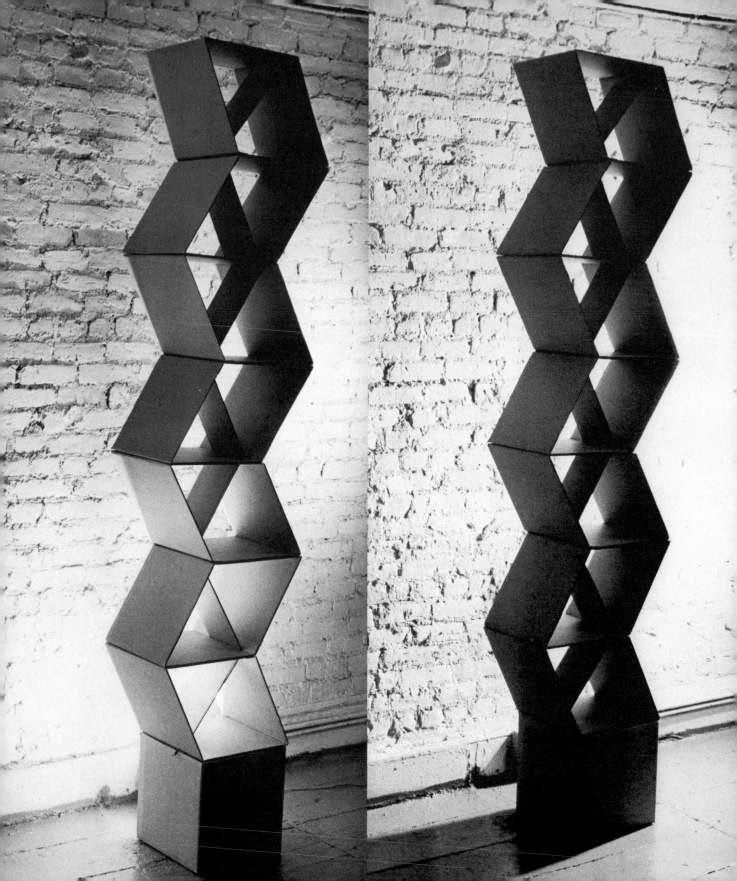

Building Big with Light

Light determines sculptural form. We cannot appreciate or build sculpture without understanding the role light plays in the plastic arts.

Because most students do not work big, three-dimensional art activities do not dramatically indicate to them the tremendously important function that light fulfills in art. Art activities do not have to be elaborate or expensive in order to give students realistic experiences with sculptural light. Here, for example, junior-high-school students use cardboard boxes, ordinary lamps, and inexpensive reflectors to model with light. They could just as easily experiment with colored light as with white light. Large-scale but easily accomplished activities such as these are the best means to acquaint students with the fact that light is as much a sculptural material as marble, steel, or plastic.

Working Walls

Wall space in art rooms is almost always used for display rather than for working. While display is obviously an important extension of teaching, it is worthwhile to consider whether an art program will benefit more from using a wall for work rather than for display, at least for part of the year. There is no reason, of course, why a wall cannot be used for both purposes.

Wall space can be easily and inexpensively converted into a work-exhibition area. The wall shown in this section is made up of a number of 4-foot-by-8-foot sheets of Homosote nailed onto a brick wall and painted with white latex paint. The ½-inch Homosote is soft enough to receive pins and staples and sturdy enough to support quite heavy sculptural objects and metal picture frames. Because it is not an expensive installation, a teacher does not have to feel guilty about letting students pin and nail into it, paint over it, and generally use it as an expendable work surface.

Relief Sculptures

The modular possibilities of cardboard boxes lend themselves as readily to relief sculpture as to sculpture in the round. In some respects the student working in relief with boxes can be freer, as there are no architectural restrictions. He is confronted with a design problem more than with a structural one.

The tops and bottoms were removed from the boxes used in the relief sculptures shown here. Although the components look extremely substantial, the boxes in fact are light enough to be held in place by a surprisingly small number of straight pins pushed through the soft but rigid surface of the boxes into the Homosote wall.

While the basic module is an open-ended cube, its square definition can be easily changed to form a number of variations on the diamond shape. Boxes placed next to one another with one side of one box matching one side of the next can be grouped to form any number of interesting geometric combinations.

The possibilities for relating art to mathematics are particularly clear here.

Although they involve the simplest of means, cardboard-box reliefs can have infinite variety. Shallow boxes will produce different effects than deeper ones; the space within each open-ended box could be broken up by crosspieces; or one side of some boxes could be removed so that the basic shape is triangular, as in the upper-left-hand illustration opposite. As in all cardboard-box construction, shadows play an important role in determining the "feel" of the completed relief.

While it might seem that the sculptor has a limited range of possibilities when working with such simple forms, in fact the emphasis of a piece can be drastically changed simply by flattening the diamonds to produce a feeling of lightness and motion or by preserving a more square shape in the units and grouping them to make solid, monolithic forms.

Once again, as in all cardboard-box projects, very large relief sculptures can be achieved quite quickly even by fairly young children. The piece shown here measures over 20 feet in length and is 9 feet high.

This sculptured wall was made with the flaps that were removed from the cardboard boxes in the sculpture shown on pages 54 and 55. Each flap was used as a light baffle. Some were left as they were; others were scored and bent to produce geometric shapes with severely angled planes designed to be highlighted or cast in shadow. The scored flaps are markedly different from the others, because the shadows in the score lines and the exposed ends of the cut corrugations are distinctly emphasized. Again, the cardboard is held in place only by straight pins; no gluing or taping is necessary.

The elements involved in a wall sculpture like the one shown here can be manipulated and fixed in place so easily that a number of students can work together at the same time on its construction, arranging and rearranging each individual area to complement the others and to produce a dramatic overall composition. The surface variations produced by the light-and-shadow play characteristic of this sort of work is strongly reminiscent of cubist painting and sculpture, so this kind of art activity could effectively parallel an appreciation unit on cubism. Some elements will invariably suggest such contemporary artists as Nevelson and Duchamp, and many lively references to a wide range of art may easily result from having a wall sculpture like this in the classroom.

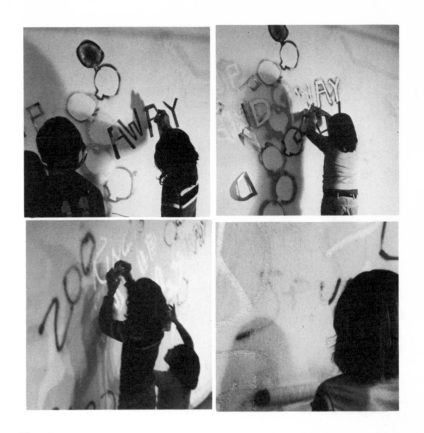

Murals
Painting a mural directly on a wall rather than on paper fastened to a wall seems more exciting and worthwhile to students. When the mural is finished and its function satisfied, a couple of coats of water-based latex paint will clear the boards for another activity.

In the photographs shown on this page junior-high-school students are using a classroom work wall to prepare movie titles, one for a film on graffiti and the other for a film about hot-air balloons. The wall had previously supported the low-relief, cardboard wall sculpture shown opposite. While work walls are especially advantageous in art programs, they also lend themselves, of course, to other subject areas.

Inexpensive, single-ply corrugated cardboard has possibilities that have not been fully realized in many art classes. This type of cardboard allows an art program with a modest budget to engage in large-scale activites that will excite student enthusiasm and invite creative work. The projects shown on these pages allow the teacher to get a great deal of mileage from one roll of this fascinating industrial product. This is yet another way to provide expansive activities with a minimum of equipment, and, because students work with no paint or glue, cleaning up is no problem.

Strips of corrugated cardboard need only to be fastened to a surface with straight pins to create very different kinds of mural effects; for example, as a basis for spray-paint murals, as a means of graphic-line presentation (such as the cartoon on page 68), or as a way to create giant designs with moiré characteristics (demonstrated on the following three pages).

Because each strip has a smooth side and a corrugated side, scintillating plays of light and shadow are possible. Light is more important to the effectiveness of this kind of art presentation than color.

As the strips are extremely lightweight and flexible, they lend themselves to design forms with a flowing, kinetic quality. Gravity becomes a design determinant, since the student can experiment with the arrangement of the points where the strips are pinned to the wall. Children become very adept at preconceiving how the material will respond if it is pinned in a certain manner.

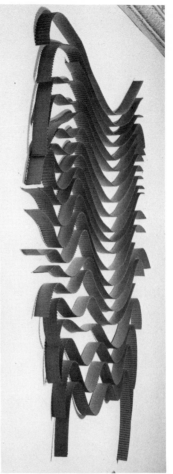

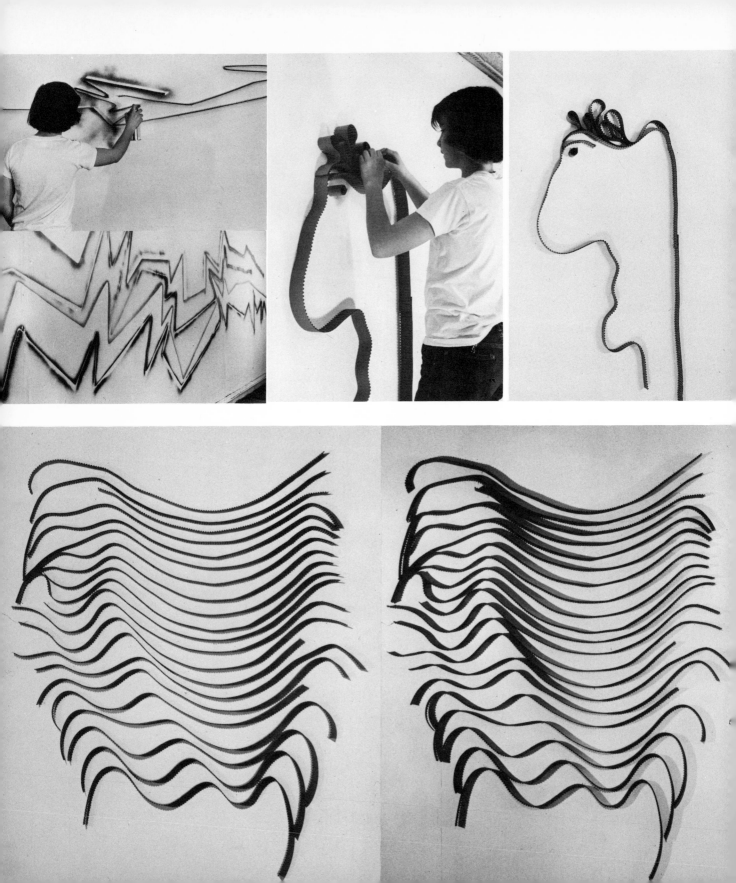

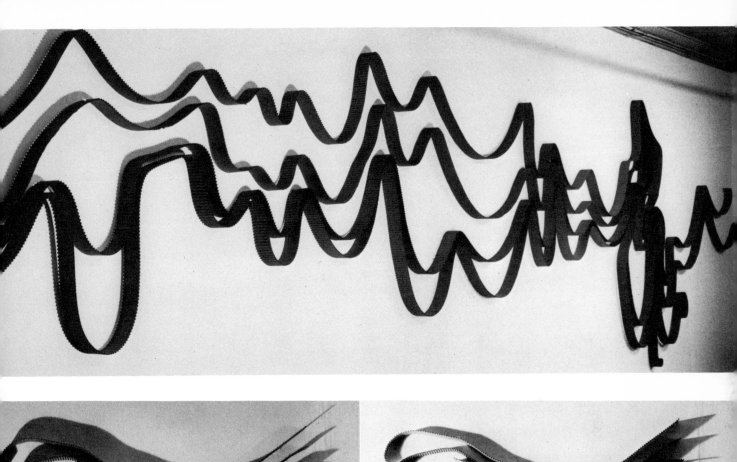

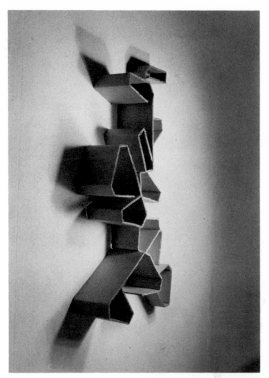

While creating his work, the sculptor cannot escape being aware of the visual impact it will have. Consciously or unconsciously, he realizes that light will be as important as material in this interaction. He is alert to the fact that shadows will make some parts of his work stand out and soften other areas so that the light and dark of his sculpture will be effective.

Either in the round or in relief, cardboard can be manipulated by creasing, bowing, or rolling it to create shadow effects that help the student sculptor achieve the overall expression of his sculptural idea.

Here we see sections taken from cardboard packing materials that have been put together to capture light and shadow and produce handsome three-dimensional forms. The only materials that were used were cardboard and the straight pins that fasten the sculpture to the wall. Once again, as in the cardboard-box sculpture, it is light that defines and clarifies the sculptor's intention.

Rolled-paper Reliefs

Rolled newspaper tubes have long been used as a basis for paper-mâché. These same tubes, however, can also be used on their own for exciting sculptural activities. Here we see them combined with wire cores in a low-relief, linear wall sculpture. Although an abstract treatment is shown, rolled newspaper can also be used to create calli-graphic forms. Because of its line quality many graphic statements are possible.

Four to six thicknesses of newspaper, each section overlapping the next, were wrapped around lengths of stovepipe wire and held in place by masking tape. Masking tape was also used to secure the tubes. Each length can be rolled around the end of the next so that the finished tube may be as long as the envisioned project requires. Because of its wire core, the student may manipulate the tubes into any shape he desires with some assurance that they will hold fast. It is best to work right on the wall, pinning each section of the design into place with straight pins as it is completed.

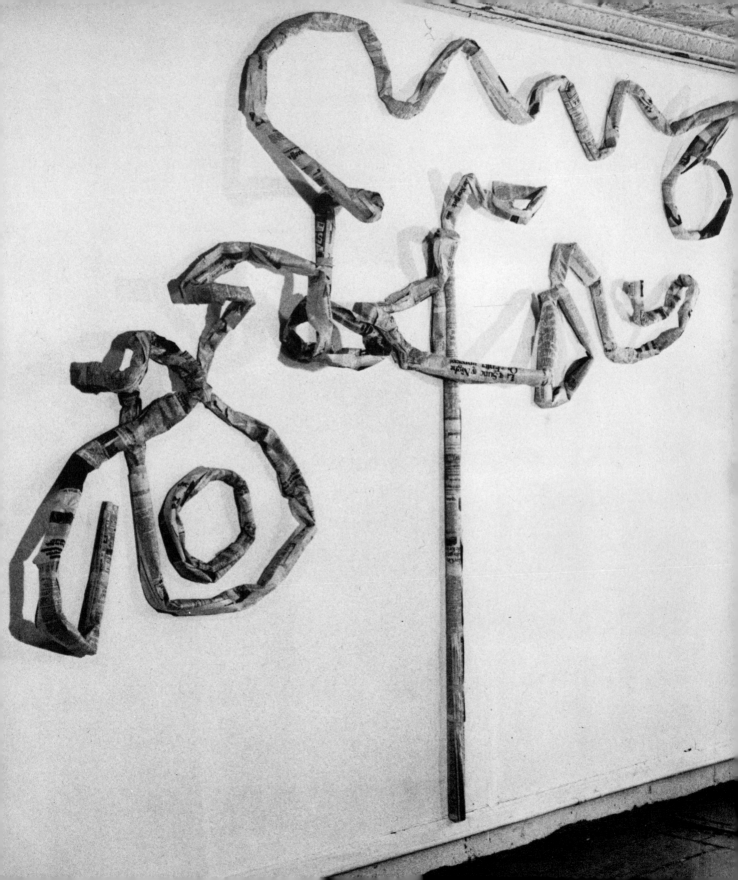

3-D Stencils

Rolled newspaper tubes are not only effective by themselves in sculpture, but they also provide an additional factor in wall stenciling. Stencils created with flat patterns tend to have a predictable cut-and-dried, hard-edge quality. When rolled newspaper is used as a three-dimensional stencil, much more imagination and subtlety can be exercised.

The artist has a great deal of freedom in working with spray paint and a rolled newspaper stencil. He can create a hard edge if he wishes, or he may blur an edge; he can keep color close to the original stencil or extend the color areas. He can achieve a line effect, or he can work in the manner of a color-field painter. He may even choose to leave the stencil intact as a raised element in his wall composition.

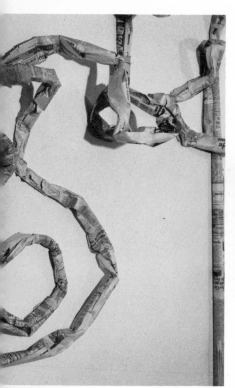
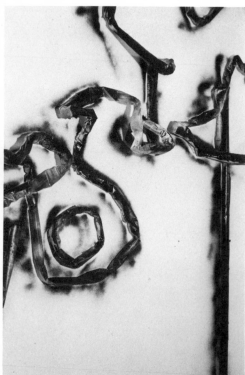

Red Grooms (left) works on cutouts for *The Discount Store,* 1970.

Cutouts

A Skilsaw plus some oversized sheets of two-ply cardboard suggest any number of big and exciting sculptural projects for junior- and senior-high-school students. Just such equipment and material prompted Red Grooms to execute *The Discount Store*. Here Danny Dobkin, an eighth-grade student at the Collegiate School in New York City, works in much the same way as Mr. Grooms with a Skilsaw and three sheets of cardboard to construct a life-size figure. The figure is, in fact, his own, traced out with a Magic Marker on the top sheet by a fellow student. The four sheets are held together by tabs of masking tape placed so they do not interfere with areas occupied by the figure itself.

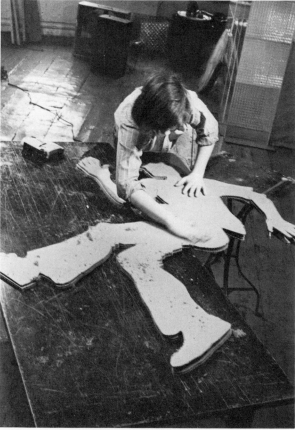

When the figure is completely sawed out, the masking tape is peeled off and the excess cardboard removed. Sawdust is brushed off, and the edges may be cleaned up with sandpaper.

The layers are separated, and both the positive figure layers and the negative shapes left over are set aside.

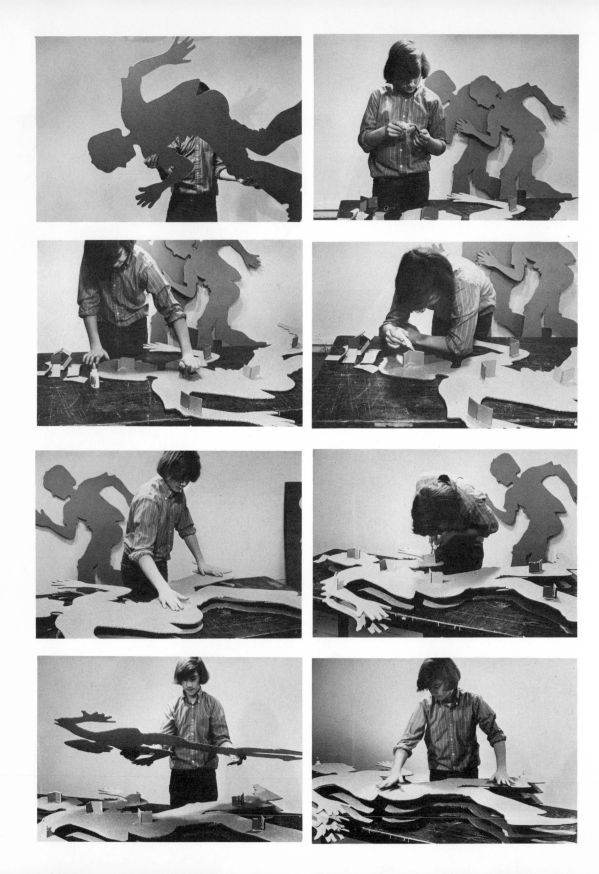

Each layer of Danny's sculpture is separated from the next by seven spacers strategically placed so they support the piece inconspicuously. The spacers are V-shaped pieces of scrap cardboard, all the same height and all placed one above another to give the sculpture architectural strength. Elmer's Glue spread on the top and bottom edges of each V secures it to the layer below and the one above. The layers are positioned so that they line up with all the others, and special care is taken to see that the bottom edges are parallel to give the figure an even base and allow it to stand up.

While Danny chose two-ply cardboard for his project, certain plastics, plywood, Styrofoam, or honeycomb board would be equally effective.

Although the natural surface of the cardboard is not unpleasant, a spray of silver paint will allow it to catch the light and emphasize its clean-cut, hard-edge quality. Spraying each layer of cardboard silver on one side and another color on the other (maybe a different color for each layer) before the sculpture is assembled will produce an interesting effect, since the color on the back of one layer will reflect on the face of the next.

This example of abstract layered sculpture is made in exactly the same way as Danny's realistic figure. Four sheets of cardboard were used instead of three, however, to emphasize the sinuous nature of the design. Lights were placed behind it and angled so that they would reflect off the many edges of the sculpture to point up its linear quality and reiterate its complexities.

The same sculpture takes on an entirely different character when a strip of corrugated cardboard is glued and pinned in place to hide its edges. Kleenex and a 50-percent solution of Elmer's Glue scumbled on its surfaces give it a heavy, solid feeling. A metallic spray increases the illusion of massive weight by suggesting that it is in fact metal.

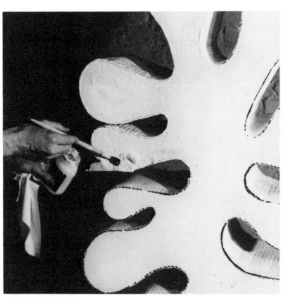

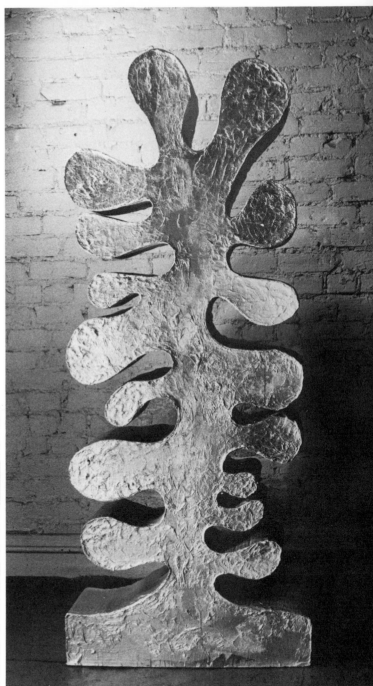

Sawed-off cardboard has an exact quality that lends itself to multiple sculpture. The sides of both units of the sculpture shown here were cut with a Skilsaw from the four sides of a discarded cardboard carton. The edges are strips of corrugated cardboard glued and pinned into place. Everything fits so beautifully that from any angle the sculpture has all the precision of a similar piece cut from steel or acrylic. Although it appears substantial and solid, each column is an extremely light cardboard shell — so light, in fact, that it is held in place by no more than two or three straight pins. The base is an ordinary cardboard box filled with old magazines. As the photographs show, the 5-foot columns may be set in various positions so that the curved outlines can interact with one another in multiple ways.

Even though the face of one column appears black while the other appears gray, in reality the cardboard was untouched. Because the columns are a few inches apart, it is possible to leave one unit in deep shadow while the other is highlighted.

Working Big Outdoors

We tend to think of ink and paint as art materials and paper and canvas as artists' working surfaces and not to think of sand and rocks, and beaches and mountainsides in the same way. Yet many contemporary artists welcome any and all materials as acceptable media and any kind of space, including the sky, as artists' space.

Environmental art and *earthworks* are considered to be recently developed forms of expression, yet both have their antecedents in such archaeological phenomena as the Irish Great Mound at Rathcroghan, neolithic in origin; the Iron Age White Horse near Uffington on the Berkshire Downs in England; and the Indian burial mounds of this country. Nature has long been recognized as the inspiration for art, but here we find that nature itself is physically central to the artist's purpose. Below, students of the City of Birmingham Polytechnic, England, participate in environmental-art activities.

Just as nature, both wild and urban, can provide the contemporary artist with inspiration as well as with the site and materials for his work, so can it provide for the creative needs of the contemporary child. In fact, the eventlike way in which the child structures his self-initiated forms of expression are uniquely accommodated by the out-of-doors. Children love to explore, to collect, to build, to be physically active — all elements of an effective art activity that can be realized through nature.

Among the more practical advantages of working with children outdoors is that the materials involved may cost little or nothing — a sculpture made from tree branches, a pattern traced in the sand, a design spelled out in pebbles, an environment of rushes and weeds, a tower reminiscent of Watts constructed of junk found in a vacant lot, or mosaics of sun-bleached glass. Outdoor projects can be big too and therefore memorable. Drawings scratched out with sticks in the sand can be fifty times the size of those attempted with pencil and paper in the classroom. Kites can be flown that can be seen for blocks around. Balloons can be launched that will soar to heights of over 1,000 feet. Just as the artist tries to extend his expression by stretching the boundaries that confine it, so can the art class look for new dimensions with which to extend its understanding not only of art but of the world.

There are as many ways to work big outside school as there are traditional ways to work within it. In fact, classroom activities themselves can be the inspiration for large-scale projects that take on new significance with the change in scope made possible by a move outdoors or into a hallway or gymnasium. Techniques which seem run-of-the-mill in the classroom inevitably become little less than sensational when the dimensions explode from, say, 9 inches by 12 inches to 90 feet by 120 feet!

Here we see a straight-line design problem typically tackled in the classroom by individual students working on their own with rulers, manila paper, and crayons or India ink blown up to such dimensions that a team of youngsters is needed to solve the same space-division problem. They do not use classroom-size supplies but large-scale materials that, although simple in themselves, invite exciting and dramatic designs and allow maximum freedom of invention.

Working with long strips of white dressmakers' buckram, the team here lays out a basic design. Two metal eyelets are punched through both ends of each strip with an art-room leather punch. Ordinary household nails stuck through the eyelets into the ground hold the strips taut in place. Each student besides working as a member of the team has his turn as foreman and directs the group in changing the organization of the strips into a design he himself invents. At the same time another member of the team takes his turn photographing the new design from an upper window of the school so that a visual record of each straight-line composition is available for display in the classroom. Pages 90 and 91 show photographs taken by a group of sixth-, seventh-, and eighth-grade students of their own designs.

The same activity could be carried out just as successfully on the concrete surface of a playground by using strips of inexpensive adding-machine tape and holding it in place with masking tape.

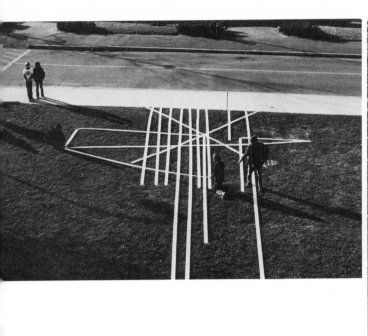

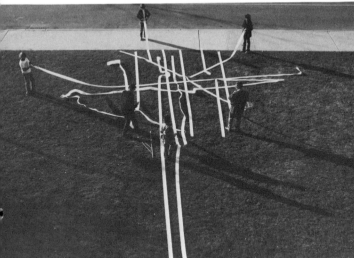

The same tapes used to create giant geometric designs are equally effective as elements in kinetic wind sculpture.

Children and Artists Work Big Together

More often than not, large-scale art projects cannot be accomplished by a single artist working on his own. If he wishes to achieve anything that exceeds a normal scale, he must plan on working as a member of a team. It is not unusual for such projects to involve a whole community. Here we see school children in Randolph, Vermont working alongside artists to produce sculpture that will become part of the community environment. While they are working in a traditional sculptor's material, marble, they are involved in the same basic experiences that children working big in the classroom enjoy.

Children who have the opportunity to work together with practicing artists and with large-scale materials are more likely to have meaningful, in-depth experiences than those whose background has been restricted to participation in small-scale classroom activities. When it is possible for children to become part of a project similar to the one we see in progress here, a school should recognize that this is not only a logical extension of the classroom curriculum but also a way that students can become involved with art forms that are relevant to the world they live in.

Eric Reische, *Untitled,* 1971. Marble. 13½ feet by 7 feet by 12½ feet.

Bibliography

Books
Lady Allen of Hurtwood. *Planning for Play*. Cambridge: MIT Press, 1974.

Baer, Steve. *Dome Cookbook*. Corrales, N. M.: Lama Cookbook Fund, 1968.

Battcock, Gregory (ed.). *New Ideas in Art Education*. New York: E. P. Dutton and Company, 1973.

Caney, Steve. *Toy Book*. New York: Workman Publishing Company, 1972.

Dattner, Richard. *Design for Play*. New York: Van Nostrand Reinhold Company, 1972.

Hurwitz, Al. *Programs of Promise*. New York: Harcourt, Brace, Jovanovich Inc., 1972.

Inflatocookbook. Sausalito: Ant Farm, 1970.

Leyh, Elizabeth. *Children Make Sculpture*. New York: Van Nostrand Reinhold Company, 1972.

Montgomery, Chandler. *Art for Teachers of Children: Foundations of Aesthetic Experience* (second edition). Columbus, Ohio: Charles E. Merrill Publishing Company, 1973.

Piene, Otto. *More Sky*. Cambridge: MIT Press, 1970.

Reichardt, Jasia (ed.). *Play Orbit*. New York: Studio International, 1969.

Articles
Bunch, Clarence and Lidstone, John. "Blow-up Space." *Athene,* vol. 16, no. 1, Spring, 1973.

Coron, Ruth Heller. "Art in the Public Domain: Transformations on a Soho Street." *Art Teacher,* vol. 4, no. 2, Spring, 1974.

Exhibition Catalogs
Sharp, Willoughby and McClanahan, Preston (eds.). *Air Art*. New York: Kineticism Press, 1968.

Journals
Art Teacher. John J. Mahlman, editor. National Art Education Association, 1916 Association Drive, Reston, Virginia 22091.

Athene. Dan Pavey, editor. Jasc House, 30 Wayside, East Sheen, London SW14 7LN, England.

Organizations
Action-Space. 89C Fitzjohn Avenue, London NW3, England.

Eventstructure Research Group. Javastraat 126, Amsterdam, Holland.

Inter-action Trust. 156 Malden Road, London NW5, England.

Acknowledgments

The authors are grateful to the following persons and organizations for their cheerful cooperation and help, without which *Working Big* would not have been possible:

Action-Space, London
Eventstructure Research Group, Amsterdam
Mrs. William H. Fredricks, Newark Museum
Sue Grayson, Director, Serpentine Gallery, London
Dr. Jay Hardwick, New Lincoln School, New York
Inter-Action Trust, London
New Forms in Art Education class, Queens College
Otto Piene, Massachusetts Institute of Technology
Eddie Price, City of Birmingham Polytechnic, England
Walker Art Center, Milwaukee
John Wittenberg, sculptor

Dr. Richard Barter, Headmaster and Ricky Barter, Brooks Bitterman, Bruce Diker, Dan Dobbin, Adam Mirim, and Courtney Ward, students at the Collegiate School, New York

Photography Credits
Action-Space, page 23
William Bowles, page 47
Mircea Campeaunu, page 3
Eventstructure, pages 22, 27
Galerie Denise René, page 48
Guardian, page 47
Dr. Jay Hardwick, page 45
John Benton Harris, pages 6–7
Ernie Hearlon, New York Times, pages 4–5
London Times, page 86
Michael Lloyd, page 1
Bob Lyon, page 20
Ron McCormick, pages 94, 95
Lynn Parisi, pages 14, 96–97
Eric Pollitzer, page 11
Eddie Price, page 87
Serpentine Gallery, cover pages, 16, 17
Eric Sutherland, page 76
Abner Symons, page 18
Walker Art Center, page 76
Andrew Watson, page 12
John Weber Gallery, pages 8, 9
John Wittenberg, pages 92, 93